What Is It?

Daniel Swartz and Jan Swartz

Illustrated by Pamela Pettigrew-Norquist

DOMINIE PRESS
Pearson Learning Group

Copyright © 2002 by Pearson Education, Inc., publishing as Dominie Press, an imprint of Pearson Learning Group, 299 Jefferson Road, Parsippany, NJ 07054.

All rights reserved. No part of this book may be reproduced or transmitted in any form or by any means, electronic or mechanical, including photocopying, recording, or by any information storage and retrieval system, without permission in writing from the publisher. For information regarding permission(s), write to Rights and Permissions Department.

ISBN 1-56270-467-2

Printed in Singapore
3 4 5 6 7 8   07 06 05

1-800-321-3106
www.pearsonlearning.com

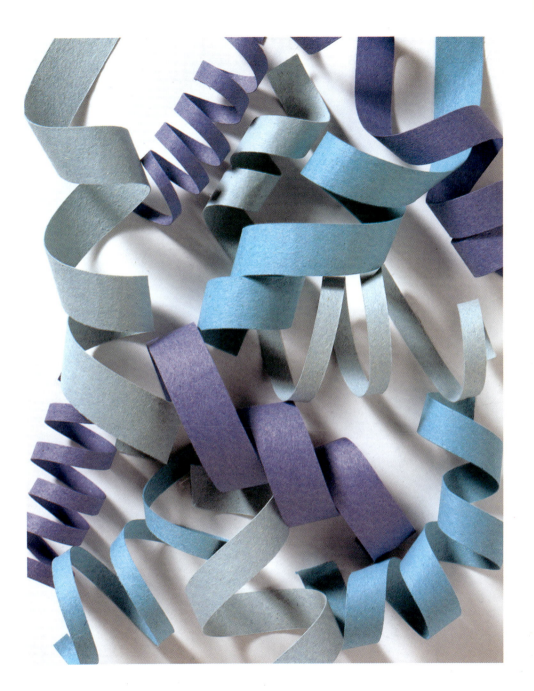

What is blue?

The sky is blue.

The water is blue.

This bird is blue.

This flower is blue.

This fish is blue.

This bike is blue.

And I am blue.